Original title:
Rising from Heartache

Copyright © 2024 Swan Charm
All rights reserved.

Author: Daisy Dewi
ISBN HARDBACK: 978-9916-89-921-2
ISBN PAPERBACK: 978-9916-89-922-9
ISBN EBOOK: 978-9916-89-923-6

From Shadow to Serenity

In the valley of shadows, hope flickers dim,
Light breaks the silence, with a soft hymn.
The heart finds its solace, in faith's gentle glow,
Guided by whispers, where love tends to grow.

From doubts that entangle, we seek to be free,
Grace calls in the stillness, a path to decree.
With each step of courage, the shadows will flee,
Embracing the dawn, we find unity.

In the arms of the sacred, we rest our weary souls,
The journey unfolds, as the spirit consoles.
In moments of anguish, the light will appear,
From shadow to serenity, we conquer our fear.

The Lifting of Heavy Burdens

With each heavy burden, we find our release,
In the arms of compassion, we harvest our peace.
Through trials we wander, and heartaches we share,
Finding strength in our weakness, we learn how to care.

The load that we carry, too great for one heart,
In the warmth of connection, we each play a part.
For every lament, there's a voice like a song,
Together we rise, where we all can belong.

As the dawn breaks anew, heavy chains turn to dust,
In love's endless promise, we flourish, we trust.
So let go of the weight, in surrender we learn,
In the lifting of burdens, the spirit will burn.

Echoes of Mercy

In the stillness of prayer, echoes whisper near,
Calls for generosity, hearts open sincere.
Each act of compassion, a ripple in time,
Resounding through ages, a love so sublime.

Forgiveness is grace, a soft hand to extend,
In the fabric of kindness, we find we transcend.
For every gentle touch that we offer with care,
As echoes of mercy, they linger in air.

In the tapestry woven, each thread plays its role,
Together we dance, as the heavens console.
In moments of struggle, let kindness unfurl,
As we mirror the light, transformed by the world.

A Testament of Triumph

Upon the mountains raised, we stand bold and free,
Chasing dreams forged in fire, our spirits decree.
With faith in our hearts, we rise from the fall,
A testament of triumph, we answer the call.

Through storms that may rage, we won't break or bend,
With courage as armor, our journey won't end.
Each challenge faced head-on, a chance to renew,
Together we rise, in the strength we pursue.

Hand in hand, united, our voices will soar,
A symphony of hope, like waves on the shore.
For every silent struggle, we sing loud and long,
In the testament of triumph, we write our own song.

Miracles Born from Mourning

Out of sorrow's depths, new hope will rise,
In the silent night, a soft voice sighs.
Tears watered seeds of grace untold,
From ashes and pain, a story unfolds.

In every heartbreak, a lesson waits,
The soul learns to heal as love elevates.
With faith as our blanket against the cold,
Miracles emerge, in whispers bold.

Spiritual Uplift: Heartstrings Unfurled

Heartstrings unfurl like petals in bloom,
In the stillness of prayer, dispelling the gloom.
Voices of angels, sweet hymns in the air,
Lift us to heights, our burdens laid bare.

In the warmth of kindness, we find our way,
Guided by light, we won't go astray.
The spirit rejoices in unity's grace,
Connected by love, we embrace His face.

Light Beyond the Shadows

In shadows that dance, there glimmers a light,
A beacon of hope piercing through the night.
With each whispered prayer, the darkness retreats,
Faith's gentle touch in every heartbeat.

The path may be steep, yet we walk hand in hand,
With love as our compass, we make our stand.
Through valleys of doubt, we carry our flame,
For in unity's warmth, we rise up again.

Serenade of Renewal

The dawn brings a melody, soft and anew,
Nature rejoices, and so should we too.
With each breath we take, a chance to renew,
In the arms of the morn, the heart starts to bloom.

Whispers of grace dance upon the breeze,
Healing our wounds, bringing souls to ease.
In the serenade sung by the trees,
We find our reflection, in love's gentle tease.

The Bridge of Faith

In shadows deep, the heart will yearn,
A light that shines, for which we turn.
With every step, on this path we tread,
The bridge of faith, where we are led.

Through trials storm, and silent plea,
A whisper soft, come follow Me.
With open arms, the spirits call,
In trust, we rise, and never fall.

Each doubt we face, a lesson learned,
In love's embrace, the soul discerned.
The journey long, yet hearts will soar,
For faith ignites, forevermore.

Resting in Divine Embrace

In gentle peace, our spirits rest,
In Divine arms, we are most blessed.
A haven found, where souls entwine,
In silence deep, His love will shine.

With every breath, a sacred sigh,
We find our strength, to rise on high.
In trust we dwell, in light we bask,
All burdens lifted, no need to ask.

The heart unites, in sacred grace,
In quiet moments, we find our place.
With gratitude, our voices raise,
In Divine love, we sing His praise.

The Power of Wounded Grace

In brokenness, our hearts reveal,
The strength that lies in wounds we heal.
Through trials fierce, we find our way,
In wounded grace, we learn to stay.

Each scar we bear, a story told,
Of battles fought, and spirits bold.
In faith we trust, through darkest night,
Wounded grace becomes our light.

The hands that mend, are hands once scarred,
With love that heals, and souls unmarred.
In every tear, a glimmer bright,
A testament to love's true might.

Miracles Born from Grief

In depths of sorrow, hope takes flight,
With heavy hearts, we seek the light.
From grief's embrace, new strength appears,
In tears we sow, our faith in years.

For every loss, a lesson learned,
Through pain we rise, and love is earned.
In shadows cast, our spirits bloom,
From grief's deep soil, miracles loom.

With open hearts, we share our pain,
In unity, our souls remain.
For from the ashes, hope will gleam,
Miracles born, from every dream.

When Sorrow Meets the Sacred

In shadows deep, we seek the light,
A whisper soft, within the night.
Each tear we shed, a prayer takes flight,
When sorrow meets the sacred sight.

With heavy hearts, we find our way,
Through trials faced, we bend and sway.
The dawn will break, and hope will stay,
Embracing love, come what may.

The sacred dance of pain and grace,
Unfolds within this holy space.
In every loss, we find our place,
In sorrow's arms, we still embrace.

For in the dark, the stars will shine,
A gentle hand, a love divine.
Through every ache, we intertwine,
In sacred trust, our spirits align.

The Altar of Resilience

Bowed but unbroken, we rise again,
With hearts aglow, we carry the pain.
On this altar, we place our shame,
Transforming strife into a name.

With every tear, a strength is born,
From ashes gray, a spirit worn.
We stand in faith, our spirits sworn,
In the fires of life, we are reborn.

Through stormy nights and trials tough,
We find the strength, we are enough.
With loving hands, when times get rough,
The altar of resilience is love.

In unity, our voices blend,
In prayerful hearts, we mend and tend.
With every step, we shall defend,
A spirit bold, until the end.

Chains Turned to Wings

From chains that bind, we seek to soar,
In faith we find the strength to explore.
Through trials faced, we break down doors,
Transforming pain into our core.

With heavy hearts, we lift our song,
In perfect trust, we will belong.
While shadows fade, we march along,
With love as our guide, we shall be strong.

Beyond the limits, we rise anew,
With every breath, our hopes break through.
From chains that grip, we're born and true,
Wings spread wide, we are the few.

To fly above, we shed our fears,
In joy we spark, with honest tears.
In faith we climb, through all the years,
Chains turned to wings, in love's sweet spheres.

The Blessing of New Beginnings

A dawn unfolds, with colors bright,
In whispered prayers, we seek the light.
With faith anew, we take our flight,
The blessing found in morning's sight.

In every end, a chance awaits,
To step beyond, to open gates.
With open hearts, we break our fates,
And walk with grace, as love creates.

With gentle hands, we weave our dreams,
In every struggle, hope redeems.
Through trials faced, we mend the seams,
The blessing of new beginnings gleams.

So let us rise, with courage bold,
In every moment, stories told.
With joy entwined, our spirits hold,
The blessing new, a promise gold.

The Light Within the Ruins

Amidst the shadows of despair,
Hope flickers like a candle's flame.
In every crack, the spirit dares,
To rise anew, in love's great name.

The ruins speak of battles lost,
Yet grace is woven through the stone.
Each echo whispers of the cost,
A heart transformed, no longer lone.

Beneath the weight of endless night,
A spark ignites within the soul.
With faith as guide, we seek the light,
Through darkened paths, we become whole.

In every tear, a story told,
Of journeys walked, of trials faced.
The sacred fire, both bright and bold,
Illuminates the sacred place.

So let the ruins fade from view,
As love constructs anew the way.
In every heart, the light shines through,
Transcending time, both night and day.

A Testament Written in Tears

Tears fall like rain from weary eyes,
Each drop a prayer, a mournful song.
In sorrow's depths, the spirit cries,
Yet from such pain, we learn to be strong.

Every wound bears a sacred grace,
A testament to love's embrace.
Through trials faced, we find our place,
In tears, the healing we must chase.

With every sigh, the heart unplugs,
The burdens borne in silence deep.
Yet in the dark, the spirit tugs,
Towards hope's promise; we shall leap.

Each tear a story, each drop a tale,
Of struggles fought and faith retained.
Through stormy seas, we shall not pale,
For love remains, forever gained.

So gather up the tears you've shed,
And write a chronicle of grace.
In every heartbeat, fear will spread,
Yet strength will rise, and love embrace.

The Sacred Echo of Awakening

In silent dawn, a whisper stirs,
The echo of the soul's refrain.
Awakening, as life concurs,
To dance with joy amidst the pain.

Each moment breathes a sacred vow,
To rise again, to break the chains.
In every heartbeat, here and now,
The spirit shouts through joy and rains.

The mountain speaks, the river flows,
In nature's hymn, our hearts align.
The sacred echo gently grows,
A tune composed by love divine.

Through every trial, the heart expands,
Embracing light in shadowed lands.
In unity, we join our hands,
In sacred space, where hope withstands.

Awake, awake, O weary soul,
The dawn awaits with open arms.
In love, we find our perfect whole,
Through every breath, the spirit warms.

The Serpent's Coil Unbound

In shadows deep, the serpent lies,
With whispered lies that pierce the skies.
Its coils embrace the heart in fear,
Yet faith can break what seems so near.

With prayers of light, we seek to rise,
Untangling truth from cloudy skies.
The chains of sin, we cast away,
In love's embrace, we find the way.

Through trials faced, our spirits grow,
In grace, we find the strength to show.
The serpent's grip, now loosed and torn,
In freedom's light, we are reborn.

With steadfast hearts, we walk the path,
From fear and doubt, we turn our wrath.
In unity, we sing, we stand,
Together bound by God's own hand.

So let the serpent coil no more,
For love has opened Heaven's door.
With every prayer, we rise and sing,
In God's embrace, we find our wing.

Pilgrimage from Pain to Peace

With heavy hearts, we walk the road,
Our burdens cast, a weighty load.
Yet on this path, the sun shall shine,
In sorrow's wake, our hope aligns.

Each step we take, a prayer unfolds,
In trust, our story quietly molds.
For every tear that stains the ground,
A seed of peace shall then abound.

The valleys low, the mountains high,
In every struggle, we learn to fly.
With faith as guide, we journey forth,
From shadows dark to inner worth.

Through trials faced, our spirits soar,
In pain, we find what we endure.
The pilgrimage, a sacred quest,
From anguish found, to quiet rest.

So let each heart, in pain believe,
That every wound can come to cleave.
In peace we find the path unveiled,
From pain to joy, our spirits hailed.

Blessings in the Midst of Sorrow

In nights of grief, when silence reigns,
We seek the light through woven chains.
Yet even in the darkest hour,
A flicker shines, a hopeful flower.

For every loss, a strength appears,
In blessings found through hidden tears.
The heart may break, but love remains,
In sorrow's wake, His grace sustains.

From ashes born, new life shall breathe,
In every wound, a chance to heave.
Though storms may rage, we find our balm,
In faith's embrace, we grow so calm.

Through trials vast, our spirits mend,
In every sorrow, a hand to lend.
With gratitude, we rise above,
In every heart, eternal love.

So in the midst of pain, we see,
The hidden blessings set us free.
With open arms, we greet the day,
In sorrow's light, we find our way.

Transfiguration of the Weeping Heart

In shadows cast, the heart does weep,
A silent cry, a promise deep.
Yet tears are not the end of song,
For in our grief, the weak grow strong.

The weeping heart shall one day bloom,
In light of love that fills the room.
Transfigured pain, a sacred thread,
In every tear, a prayer is said.

Through trials fierce, our hearts ignite,
With every anguish, we find the light.
In transformation, wounds do heal,
Our spirits rise, our souls reveal.

The journey long, yet hope remains,
In all the hurt, the joy sustains.
With open hearts, we greet the dawn,
Transfigured souls, from night till morn.

So let the weeping heart unfold,
In grace, the story shall be told.
With love anew, we rise apart,
In every tear, a healing heart.

The Light That Draws Us Home

In the quiet night, a star does gleam,
Guiding our hearts toward a sacred dream.
With every step, the shadows fade,
In faith we walk, unafraid.

Whispers of hope fill the air we breathe,
A promise made, in love we believe.
Each moment shines, like dawn's first light,
Drawing us close, dispelling the night.

Through trials faced, through valleys low,
The beacon shines, its warmth we know.
In unity, our spirits rise,
Together we seek, where true peace lies.

The path is clear, the goal in sight,
With open hearts, we embrace the light.
As one we journey, hand in hand,
To the sacred shores of a promised land.

A Covenant with Tomorrow

In the dawn's embrace, we find our way,
A pact awaits in the light of day.
With each heartbeat, a promise made,
To nurture hope, never to fade.

The whispers of faith call through the trees,
Binding our spirits, like a gentle breeze.
With open arms, we greet the morn,
A future bright, where love is born.

Through trials and test, we shall endure,
With faith our shield, our hearts secure.
In every choice, let grace abide,
With love as our guide, forever side by side.

Together we stand, in purpose strong,
Building a world where all belong.
In each tomorrow, a chance to thrive,
In this sacred bond, we come alive.

The Blessing of the Broken

In shadows deep, where pain resides,
A whisper calls, where hope abides.
Through every crack, the light breaks through,
In love's embrace, we find anew.

The scars we bear tell stories true,
Of battles fought, of kindness too.
In brokenness, we learn to see,
The beauty birthed in vulnerability.

Each tear a testament, each sigh a prayer,
For in our wounds, we learn to care.
With open hands, we share our grace,
In every heart, a sacred space.

Together we rise, together we stand,
In unity's strength, we make our plans.
Through trials faced, we find our song,
In the blessing of the broken, we belong.

A Journey Through Sacred Shadows

Through shadows cast, we tread the path,
With courage held against the wrath.
Our hearts ignited by faith's embrace,
In quiet moments, we find our place.

The stars above, a guiding light,
Illuminate our steps through the night.
In sacred whispers, we hear the call,
To rise and stand, to never fall.

With every heartbeat, we seek the truth,
In the tapestry woven since our youth.
Each step a lesson, each turn a chance,
To dance in grace, to sing and dance.

As shadows fade, we hold the flame,
Transcending fears, we find our name.
In unity's light, we journey on,
In sacred shadows, our hope is strong.

Embracing Tomorrow's Dawn

As the sun breaks through the night,
Hope ignites, a gentle light.
Casting shadows far away,
We rise anew with each new day.

In the heavens, angels sing,
Of the joys that morning brings.
With every whisper, peace descends,
A promise that the dawn defends.

Our weary hearts in faith shall soar,
To greet the grace forevermore.
Embracing paths that lie ahead,
With love's embrace, our fears will shed.

In the stillness of the morn,
Our spirits stretch, awakened, born.
Through trials faced, we find our way,
Embracing tomorrow's bright display.

For in every blade of grass,
The light of hope shall ever pass.
With open arms, we greet the day,
And in His light, forever stay.

Divine Renewal: A Soul's Journey

Upon the road where souls do tread,
Each step a prayer, a light that's spread.
In silent whispers, truth unfolds,
A journey woven in love's holds.

Mountains rise and rivers flow,
Guiding paths to where we grow.
With faith as our unwavering guide,
In divine renewal, we confide.

Through valleys deep and in the night,
We seek the grace, the sacred light.
With every tear, a lesson learned,
In love's embrace, our hearts are turned.

In the temple of the spirit's might,
We find our strength, our inner fight.
For in each moment's soft caress,
A soul's renewal brings us blessedness.

As dawn breaks over every trial,
We journey forth with hopeful smile.
In every step, the light shall rise,
In divine renewal, our souls shall thrive.

Lifting the Weary Soul

When burdens weigh on hearts so tight,
And shadows linger, dimming light.
A hand extended, gentle, warm,
Shall lift the weary through the storm.

In sacred silence, prayers ascend,
Calling forth the peace we send.
With each soft breath, in trust, we seek,
To find the strength when we are weak.

For every trial shall have its end,
In faith and love, our souls transcend.
Through caring hearts, we heal the pain,
In lifting others, kindness reigns.

With every tear, the soul shall rise,
As hope allies with the skies.
United voices, strong and whole,
We find our grace, uplifting soul.

So let us walk this path as one,
With faith that shines as bright as sun.
In unity, the weary find,
Their burdens shared, their souls aligned.

Grace After the Fall

When darkness looms and spirits break,
And fragile hearts begin to ache.
A promise whispers in the night,
That grace shall follow with the light.

For every stumble on this way,
In shadows cast, we humbly pray.
With every fall, a lesson taught,
In grace, a sacred bond is wrought.

From ashes rise, renewed once more,
With every wound, an open door.
Through trials faced, divinely small,
We learn to rise, despite the fall.

Hope blooms amidst the broken dreams,
In quiet places, love redeems.
For every tear that marks the ground,
In grace, our strength is truly found.

So let us dance upon our scars,
Embracing life beneath the stars.
For in the heart, the truth recalls,
That we are saved by grace after falls.

The Well of Forgiveness

In the depths where shadows lie,
Hearts seek solace, spirits sigh.
With every drop, a burden eased,
In this well, our souls are pleased.

Casting stones upon the shore,
Waves of mercy, evermore.
Each ripple hints at grace bestowed,
In forgiveness, love is sowed.

Gathered thoughts like autumn leaves,
Swirling softly, truth believes.
Let the past become the past,
In forgiveness, peace is cast.

Open hands, we lift in prayer,
As we free the weight we bear.
In this well, let wounds be healed,
Forgiveness given, hearts revealed.

So we drink from holy springs,
In our hearts, the songbird sings.
Through the trials we have braved,
In forgiveness, we are saved.

Ascending Through the Struggle

Upon the mountain, storm clouds loom,
Yet faith ignites the heart's warm bloom.
Step by step, we rise each day,
In struggle lies the sacred way.

Through trials fierce and tempests wild,
We are nurtured, the Spirit's child.
Every tear, a lesson learned,
In the fire, our spirits burned.

Climbing high where eagles soar,
We find strength at every door.
With hands uplifted, voices raised,
In the struggle, hope is praised.

In shadows cast, we find the light,
Our journey marked by faith and might.
For every fear, there blooms a prayer,
In ascension, love is rare.

Through the vale, our vision clears,
With every step, we face our fears.
In unity, we shall prevail,
Ascending through the stormy gale.

Renewal in the Silent Whisper

In the quiet, Spirit speaks,
In gentle tones, the heart it seeks.
Amidst the noise, we find the peace,
In silent whispers, doubts release.

Through the stillness, truth unfolds,
In soft embrace, our faith holds.
Beneath the stars that light our way,
In renewal, we humbly pray.

As the dawn breaks, shadows flee,
With every dawn, we are set free.
In the silence, hearts entwine,
With every breath, the divine shines.

Nature's song, a sacred tune,
In every leaf, and every moon.
Whispers carry, secrets shared,
In renewal, we are bared.

With open hearts, we hear the call,
In the silent, we're free from all.
Through every moment, pure and bright,
In the whisper, we find our light.

The Divine Thread of Strength

Woven tightly, faith's embrace,
In trials faced, we find our place.
A golden thread that binds us tight,
In darkness, it becomes our light.

Through every storm, we seek the path,
In every sorrow, love's sweet wrath.
With threads of hope, we stitch our fate,
In unity, we elevate.

Strong as mountains, brave as seas,
The divine thread flows with ease.
Holding fast in love's great scheme,
We are threaded through the dream.

With open hearts, we find our way,
Each step taken, come what may.
In every bond, divinity's hand,
The thread of strength in life's demand.

So let us weave our stories bright,
In the fabric of pure light.
Through every tear, through every laugh,
The divine thread guides our path.

Blossoms from the Broken

In gardens where shadows dwell,
Resilience whispers, all is well.
From cracked soil, new life shall spring,
Hope's gentle touch, a sacred thing.

The tears we shed, like morning dew,
Nourishing dreams, both bright and true.
From ashes rise, the spirit's song,
In brokenness, we find where we belong.

Through trials faced, our faith refines,
In every loss, God's love defines.
The heart's deep ache, a holy seed,
In struggle's grasp, we find our creed.

Each petal soft, with grace bestowed,
In pain and strife, the truth unveiled.
The blossoms bloom where hope has cried,
With every breath, we rise, abide.

Within the cracks, a light does gleam,
Guiding the soul towards the dream.
From broken paths, a journey new,
In every heart, a miracle true.

A Pilgrimage of the Heart

Upon the road where faith begins,
Each step is woven with the sins.
In shadows deep, the soul is led,
To find the light, the heart must tread.

The whispers of a sacred prayer,
Guide weary feet through storms of care.
With each encounter, a lesson learned,
The heart ignites, its passion burned.

Through valleys low and mountains high,
God's gentle hand, our spirit's sky.
In moments still, we hear the call,
In every rise, we learn to fall.

The road is long, yet filled with grace,
In every heart, we find our place.
With open arms, we share the love,
A holy bond, ordained from above.

Onward we walk, through joys and strife,
In every heartbeat, echoes of life.
A pilgrimage that never ends,
The heart's own path, where spirit blends.

The Light After the Storm

When tempests roar and shadows play,
The heart finds strength, come what may.
In darkest nights, a spark appears,
A guiding star to calm our fears.

With faith as anchor, souls prevail,
Through stormy seas, love's vibrant trail.
The dawn will break, the skies will clear,
In every tear, the light draws near.

Each trial faced, a lesson taught,
In battles fought, a hope once sought.
The rainbow bends, a promise true,
In every heart, the light shines through.

A whisper soft, a gentle breeze,
Brings solace to the soul's unease.
In gratitude, we stand renewed,
In every moment, God's grace pursued.

After the storm, peace reigns inside,
With open hearts, we'll not hide.
Together, we embrace the day,
For love endures; it lights the way.

Embracing the Holy Transformation

In chrysalis, the spirit waits,
The folds of grace, where change creates.
A dance of light upon the soul,
With every breath, we become whole.

In trials faced, we shed the past,
Emerging strong, our hearts steadfast.
The sacred fire ignites the night,
Transforming pain into pure light.

With open arms, we greet the dawn,
Each shadow cast, a lesson drawn.
Through struggles deep, we learn to see,
In every end, new life shall be.

The joy of change, a holy breath,
In life's embrace, there is no death.
With faith as guide, we journey forth,
In every heart, a sacred birth.

Each step we take, a prayer extends,
With love's compassion, the soul mends.
Transformation's grace, our truest fate,
In every heart, we celebrate.

Ascension of the Broken Spirit

In shadows deep where sorrows weep,
A spirit bruised seeks solace steep.
Rising up from dust and pain,
Faith's gentle whisper calls again.

The weight of tears, a heavy crown,
Yet love's embrace will not let down.
From brokenness, a light shines forth,
Each weary step reveals new worth.

A prayer ascends with every breath,
Transcending trials, conquering death.
With wings of grace, the heart takes flight,
In the dawn, behold the light.

The journey long, through valleys low,
Yet hope's sweet song begins to grow.
For every wound that seemed a loss,
Is healed in faith, beneath the cross.

Ascended high, the spirit free,
In unity with all that be.
From pain to peace, in love we bind,
A testament of the divine mind.

From Ashes to the Light

In the depth of night, where shadows cling,
The soul, like a phoenix, begins to sing.
From ashes cold, the fire ignites,
To journey forward, embrace the heights.

Each heartache faced, a lesson learned,
Through trials fierce, the spirit burned.
Yet from the wreckage, hope will rise,
Like morning dew beneath clear skies.

Faith is the spark that lights the flame,
In every loss, we can reclaim.
Through every ache that sought to steal,
Resilience builds, and wounds can heal.

The path is long, the road is wide,
But love will walk steadfast beside.
In every tear, a promise flows,
To lead us where the pure heart knows.

From ashes dark, the dawn appears,
With joyful hearts, we cast our fears.
In light we find our way to thrive,
For in this grace, we are alive.

The Resurrection of Hope

In the grave of doubt, where dreams decay,
A seed of hope still finds its way.
Through darkened roads, it bends and breaks,
And from the void, a new path wakes.

In silent prayers, the heart does yearn,
For every flame that seeks to burn.
Resurrection blooms in tender grace,
Revealing beauty in every place.

Hope is the anchor in raging seas,
It whispers soft on the gentle breeze.
With every challenge, it grows more bold,
A testament of stories untold.

Life's fleeting moments hold sacred space,
In every trial, we find our place.
The heart resurrects with every tear,
Embracing love that's ever near.

From every loss, a treasure found,
In faith and love, we are unbound.
The risen hope in every heart,
A sacred bond, never to part.

Hymn of the Healing Heart

When shadows fall and hearts feel cold,
A healing hymn begins to unfold.
In every note, a whisper true,
The balm of mercy will renew.

With gentle hands, the spirit mends,
Each broken piece, the Father sends.
A symphony of grace takes flight,
Transforming darkness into light.

The healing waters flow divine,
In every soul, a sacred sign.
With every beat, the heart does sing,
A song of peace the angels bring.

Through trials faced, we find the way,
At dawn's first light, we see the day.
For love will cleanse, and hope will heal,
In every breath, we find what's real.

Hymn of the heart, forever raised,
In gratitude, our souls are praised.
From pain to joy, we dance anew,
In harmony, we are made true.

In the Stillness of the Spirit

In the quiet hush of dawn,
Whispers call from realms above.
Hearts align in gentle grace,
Seeking truth, entwined in love.

Paths of light stretch far and wide,
Faith a guide through shadows cast.
In the stillness, hopes abide,
Holding fast, our souls hold fast.

Each breath a prayer, sweet and pure,
In every sigh, the sacred breath.
Finding strength in the uncertain,
Transforming fears, confronting death.

Grace descends like morning dew,
Softly gracing weary minds.
Cleansing hearts, renewing sight,
In this stillness, peace we find.

So let our spirits roam the skies,
As stars ignite the vast expanse.
In the stillness of our souls,
We rise anew, a sacred dance.

The Ascendant Heart

Lifted high, the heart takes flight,
Beyond the clouds, to realms divine.
Embracing hope in love's embrace,
Ascendant spirit, brightly shine.

In trials faced, we find our strength,
Through darkest nights, the soul can soar.
With faith ignited, we ascend,
A flame that breaks through every door.

Mountains bow before the grace,
Of hearts that rise, unbound, set free.
In unity, our voices sing,
A symphony of harmony.

Through valleys low and heights unknown,
Our journey carved in sacred light.
The ascendant heart, a guiding star,
Shines through the shadows of the night.

Each pulse a prayer, each beat a song,
In luminous embrace we stand.
Together in this dance of love,
The ascendant heart, forever grand.

The Baptism of Pain to Purpose

In the fires of trials we find,
The baptism of pain so profound.
Wounds become whispers of grace,
Transforming hearts, healing the ground.

With every tear that falls like rain,
A seed of wisdom takes its root.
From shadows deep, light breaks through,
Emerging strength in sacred fruit.

The forge of anguish shapes our soul,
A crucible of love's own design.
Through trials faced, our spirits grow,
Revealing purpose, divine, divine.

As dawn breaks forth on the weary night,
Resilience blooms in every heart.
The baptism of pain transforms,
A sacred journey, where love imparts.

So let us walk with heads held high,
In unity, through fire and rain.
For every wound becomes a light,
The baptism of pain to purpose, our gain.

Resilience in the Presence of Divinity

In your light, we find our way,
A tapestry of love and grace.
Resilience woven through each thread,
In your presence, we embrace.

With every storm that shakes the soul,
Your guiding hand, our shelter strong.
In trials deep, we stand as one,
Together in this sacred song.

The heartbeat of the universe,
Sings truth within our restless core.
Your spirit moves, igniting hope,
Resilience blooms forevermore.

In the quiet moments, we find,
The strength to rise, renewed and bold.
In our hearts, your presence dwells,
A sanctuary of love untold.

So let us walk with faith and grace,
In the presence of divinity.
Resilience springs in every breath,
Together bound in unity.

A Pilgrim's Encounter with Light

In shadowed vale I walked alone,
A whisper called, a gentle tone.
The dawn appeared, a sacred sight,
Illuminating my weary plight.

With every step, the warmth did rise,
As sunbeams danced in sacred skies.
A presence filled the empty space,
I found my heart, I found His grace.

The path ahead, though rough and steep,
A promise made, in trust I leap.
With every breath, a prayer I weave,
In Light divine, I do believe.

Each moment filled with holy fire,
Awakening the deepest desire.
For in this journey, I feel alive,
In Love's embrace, my spirit thrives.

So onward I go, with hope anew,
Guided by faith, so pure and true.
In every shadow, His light I'll find,
A pilgrim's heart, forever aligned.

Season of the Renewed

As blossoms burst in vibrant hues,
The earth awakens, fresh with news.
In quiet whispers, nature sings,
Of love reborn and sacred things.

The winter's grip begins to fade,
With every ray, a promise made.
In hearts once cold, a spark ignites,
The joy of living, shining bright.

With every dawn, the spirit grows,
In fields of faith, the flower shows.
Hope dances lightly on the breeze,
A symphony of gentle ease.

The hands of time, they shift and mold,
Unfolding stories yet untold.
In every season, there's a chance,
To find our way, to learn to dance.

Now let us praise this life renewed,
In gratitude for all that's true.
For every heartbeat, every breath,
Is a testament of life, not death.

The Shimmering Path to Freedom

Beneath the weight of yesterday,
A shimmering path lights the way.
Each step I take, in faith I tread,
With hope alive, and fears all shed.

The chains that bind begin to break,
In every choice, my soul awakes.
The gentle breeze, it carries me,
To shores of peace, a vast sea.

With love as guide, I trust the flow,
Through trials faced, the truth will glow.
No longer lost, I find my ground,
On wings of spirit, freedom found.

Each moment ripe with sacred worth,
A life reborn, a second birth.
The light within, it starts to rise,
A boundless love, beyond the skies.

So let us walk this brilliant way,
With hearts ablaze, and spirits gay.
In unity, together strive,
For in this path, we truly thrive.

Symphony of the Redeemed

In harmony, the faithful sing,
A symphony of love, we bring.
Each note a prayer, each chord a plea,
A bridge of grace, from you to me.

Through valleys low and mountains high,
Together we rise, we soar, we fly.
The melodies of hearts combined,
Echo the voice of the Divine.

With every heartbeat, a rhythm starts,
Resounding love within our hearts.
In unison, we drift and sway,
An anthem carved from faith's pure clay.

As shadows fall and trials come,
In sacred song, we overcome.
For in each struggle, strength is found,
In every tear, redemption's sound.

So lift your voice, let spirits soar,
In joyous praise, forevermore.
In symphony, let us abide,
The redeemed chorus, side by side.

Within Fragile Walls: A Fortress of Faith

In shadows deep, the spirit stands,
Guarded by love, held in gentle hands.
With prayer like arrows shooting high,
We find our strength in trust, not sighs.

These fragile walls, they break and bend,
Yet peace within will never end.
Through stormy nights and sunlit days,
Our faith remains in steadfast ways.

Each crack a story, each scar a prayer,
Within this fortress, we learn to care.
Bound by the hope that never quits,
In sacred grace, our spirit fits.

Together we rise, no longer alone,
In this haven, our hearts are sown.
A refuge built on love's embrace,
Within fragile walls, we find our place.

A Journey to the Celestial Garden

Beneath the stars, we tread the light,
Each step a whisper, a holy rite.
In valleys vast, where shadows play,
We seek the dawn of a brighter day.

The garden blooms with colors bright,
A canvas painted with love's pure light.
With every petal, a promise shared,
In sacred ground, we find we're spared.

The fragrant air, so rich and warm,
Surrounds our hearts, a gentle charm.
Among the trees, our souls take flight,
In this celestial space of endless light.

A journey blessed, a path divine,
With every breath, your spirit mine.
Together we wander, hand in hand,
In the embrace of this holy land.

The Rebirth of the Unbroken

Once shattered dreams lay on the ground,
In pieces, yet hope can still be found.
With every trial, we rise anew,
From ashes born, our spirits true.

The dawn awakens, light breaks through,
In moments dark, we find the view.
Resilience grows where pain once thrived,
In every song, our hearts revived.

For every wound that time will heal,
A story told, a fate to seal.
The unbroken rise, a fierce array,
In love's embrace, we find our way.

With hearts aglow, we stand as one,
A testament to battles won.
In the rebirth, we stand so strong,
In faith and love, we all belong.

Found in the Embrace of Grace

In solitude, we seek the light,
The whispered voice in the endless night.
With open hearts, we learn to trust,
In humble submission, we find the just.

The gentle touch of a loving hand,
Softens the path like golden sand.
A shelter built on faith's embrace,
In every trial, we find our place.

Through every storm that shakes our core,
Grace lifts us high, forevermore.
In trials faced, our spirits soar,
In unity, we seek the shore.

For in fragile moments, love prevails,
Through darkest hours, our hope sets sails.
In grace we dwell, forever blessed,
United in faith, our souls find rest.

The Sacred Tapestry of Life

In shadows deep, the spirit weaves,
Threads of fate, through joys and grieves.
Each moment shines, a precious thread,
In life's grand loom, where hearts are fed.

Woven paths, both bright and dim,
Guiding souls to the light within.
With faith as gold, and love's embrace,
We find our purpose, a sacred place.

Through storms that rage, our tapestry stands,
Hand in hand, united, we make our plans.
In sacred bonds, we thrive and grow,
In every stitch, the love we sow.

From mountains high to valleys low,
The sacred story continues to flow.
Each life a strand, together they shine,
In the tapestry of the divine.

Thus cherish each thread, every kind act,
For in this weave, the truth is packed.
Our hearts entwined, a living hymn,
In this sacred dance, we learn to swim.

A Symphony of Revival

From silence deep, a voice awakes,
Through valleys low, the spirit shakes.
Resounding echoes of love's sweet grace,
In every heart, a sacred place.

Let melodies rise like morning dew,
Awakening souls, both old and new.
Each note a prayer, each harmony bright,
Guiding us through the darkest night.

With every chord, the past releases,
In gentle waves, the spirit eases.
A symphony born from pain and plight,
Transforms our fears into pure light.

Together we sing, united in strength,
In love's embrace, we find our length.
Through trials faced and battles won,
The symphony plays, our hearts outrun.

So lift your voice, let the heavens hear,
In this revival, we conquer fear.
With faith as our guide, we stand as one,
A symphony of love, forever begun.

The Vessel of Redemption

In the quiet dawn, the heart's cry yearns,
For sacred truths, the spirit learns.
A vessel found, with purpose clear,
To hold the light, and conquer fear.

Within the storm, it sails so bold,
A journey vast, as stories unfold.
Through stormy seas and waters deep,
The vessel of redemption does not sleep.

With every wave, past burdens shed,
In open arms, the light is fed.
Each tear transformed, a pearl of grace,
In this vessel, we find our place.

Forgiveness flows like rivers wide,
Washing wounds, the heart's own guide.
In warmth of love, we find our shore,
A vessel cherished, forevermore.

So sail with faith, let spirits soar,
In the vessel of redemption, we explore.
With every heartbeat, a story told,
In sacred waters, our souls unfold.

Harvesting Hope from Heartache

In fields of sorrow, we patiently sow,
Seeds of hope, where storms may blow.
From fractured dreams, we tend with care,
A garden blooms, love everywhere.

With gentle hands, we nurture grace,
In heartache's depth, we find our place.
Each tear a raindrop, a story's end,
In harvest time, the soul can mend.

Through trials faced, new strength we gain,
From every loss, a spark remains.
In quiet moments, we learn to heal,
Harvesting hope, the soul reveals.

Though shadows linger, light breaks through,
With every dawn, a vision anew.
We gather joy where pain once reigned,
In fields of heartache, love is gained.

So cherish each struggle, each fleeting hour,
For from the heartache, we rise with power.
In the garden of life, we find our way,
Harvesting hope, day by day.

Celestial Embrace of Solace

In quiet night, the stars do gleam,
A gentle touch, a sacred beam.
Whispers soft, from realms above,
Embrace us with unending love.

Beneath the moon, our fears take flight,
In shadows dim, we seek the light.
Heavenly peace, our hearts entwine,
In this embrace, the soul aligns.

Covenant of the Brave

With courage strong, we stand as one,
In trials faced, our battles won.
Guided by the flame within,
We rise anew, we will not sin.

The bond we forge, a sacred trust,
In faith we walk, in hope we must.
With every stride, the path we'll pave,
Together bound in the brave.

Prayers of a Weary Traveler

On winding roads, my spirit frail,
I seek the peace beyond the pale.
With every step, I lift my cries,
To find the truth in the skies.

The weight I bear, a heavy load,
Yet in the dark, You light the road.
O guide my heart, through storms and strife,
In prayer, I find the breath of life.

The Nectar of Redemption

In brokenness, I find my pain,
Yet through the tears, Your grace remains.
A gentle rain, the soul restored,
In every drop, Your love adored.

The sweetest balm for hearts in need,
Your nectar flows, a holy creed.
Through trials faced, my spirit sings,
In redemption's light, new life springs.

The Holy Journey Within

In silence deep, the spirit seeks,
A path of light, where wisdom speaks.
Through shadows cast, and trials faced,
We find the grace that can't be replaced.

With every step, the heart unfolds,
In faith, the truth of love it holds.
The sacred voice, a gentle guide,
As we align with Him, our stride.

Each tear we shed, a lesson learned,
In all the ways, His light has burned.
The journey long, yet blessed anew,
In every breath, we're born and grew.

Beneath the stars, our spirits soar,
In unity, we seek much more.
Together bound, we walk the line,
In sacred joy, our souls entwine.

At journey's end, we find the peace,
In love's embrace, our fears release.
The holy flame dwelling within,
A shining truth, our true begin.

The Flame of I Am

In the stillness, a fire ignites,
A whisper of truth, in darkest nights.
The essence pure, a radiant spark,
Awakening hearts, illuminating dark.

From ashes rise, the spirits bright,
Bound by love, enveloped in light.
Eternal flame, that never wanes,
In every heart, its song remains.

When shadows creep, and doubts draw near,
The flame of I Am, banishes fear.
In moments scarce, in trials of soul,
Resurgence comes, to make us whole.

With every breath, the embers grow,
A beacon of hope, as we bestow.
Each soul a light, in heaven's choir,
United we stand, in divine fire.

The journey forth, with hearts ablaze,
We walk as one, in holy praise.
Together we rise, hand in hand,
For in this flame, forever we stand.

A Celestial Resurgence

In realms above, where angels shine,
Awaits the promise, pure divine.
The call resounds, a cosmic song,
In every heart, we all belong.

Through trials faced, with faith so strong,
We find resurgence in love's sweet throng.
In silence deep, we hear the grace,
That beckons us to seek His face.

The stars align, in sacred dance,
Our spirits lift in timeless chance.
As galaxies whisper our names,
We rise anew, unbound by chains.

Each moment blessed, as time unfolds,
With love's embrace, the truth beholds.
In every heartbeat, a sacred drum,
As we awaken, we come undone.

In this union, our souls ignite,
A celestial surge, the dawn of light.
Forever changed, we walk the path,
In love unbroken, we find our faith.

When Hearts Are Made Whole

In shattered dreams, where shadows lie,
Hope flickers forth, a passion high.
From broken pieces, new life blooms,
In love's embrace, our spirit resumes.

Each heart that beats, a tale to weave,
In unity found, we dare to believe.
We hold our hands, through trials we face,
Together we rise, enveloped in grace.

With every laugh, with every tear,
The bonds grow strong, our purpose clear.
In moments shared, the light breaks through,
When hearts are made whole, we are renewed.

In love's great dance, we intertwine,
A tapestry bright, divine design.
No longer alone, we stand as one,
In this sacred place, our journey begun.

As we walk forth, with open hearts,
The sacred flame in each imparts.
When love prevails, in every soul,
We find our truth, when hearts are whole.

Threads of Grace in the Tapestry of Life

In weaving light through darkest night,
Threads of grace take gentle flight.
Each moment stitched with faith and trust,
In every heart, His love is just.

The colors blend, a sacred sign,
In every struggle, His hands align.
A tapestry where souls entwine,
The pattern formed, forever divine.

In joys bestowed and sorrows shared,
Every thread shows how we cared.
With hopeful eyes, we see His plan,
United in grace, together we stand.

Through trials faced and victories won,
The fabric grows with each new dawn.
In gratitude, we lift our praise,
For love upheld in countless ways.

So trust the weaver's skilled design,
In every knot, His light will shine.
Threads of grace throughout all strife,
In the grand tapestry of life.

The Quiet Rise of a Faithful Heart

In silence deep, the spirit sings,
A faithful heart, where love takes wings.
Amidst the noise, it finds its way,
To rise in hope with each new day.

With patient hands, it holds the light,
Guiding souls through darkest night.
In whispered prayers, its strength is found,
A gentle spirit, forever bound.

In valleys low and mountains high,
The faithful heart will never die.
It weaves its truth through trials faced,
A testament to love embraced.

With every step, it walks in grace,
Unfolding peace, a warm embrace.
Its quiet rise, a beacon bright,
Leading hearts from night to light.

So let it soar, this heart so true,
In every moment, it brings anew.
A faithful heart shall never part,
Embracing love, a sacred art.

Metaphors of Liberation

In chains of fear, we once were bound,
Yet faith arose, and hope was found.
Like birds that soar in skies so wide,
Our spirits free, with Christ as guide.

The storm may rage, the night may fall,
But love persists, it conquers all.
With every tear, a seed is sown,
In brokenness, new strength has grown.

We cast aside the weight we bear,
In trusting hands, we lay our care.
Metaphors of light and grace,
In every heart, we find our place.

From prison cells to open skies,
In faith, the spirit always flies.
Through shadows deep, we march as one,
With every step, the battle won.

So let us rise on wings of hope,
Through every trial, we learn to cope.
In metaphors of love we stand,
Liberated, hand in hand.

Shattered Chains

The chains of doubt begin to break,
In faith we rise, for love's own sake.
In every struggle, freedom calls,
As broken hearts, His mercy falls.

With courage fierce, we step ahead,
In light of truth, our fears are shed.
The past behind, a new dawn's light,
The chains are shattered, taking flight.

From ashes rise a spirit bold,
A story of redemption told.
In every wound, the healing starts,
Shattered chains, united hearts.

We walk in grace, on paths anew,
With every step, His love shines through.
The weight released, we'll dance in praise,
For in our hearts, His hope we raise.

So let us sing with joyous cheer,
For shattered chains no longer near.
In faith we stand, forever free,
A testament to His decree.

Gentle Whispers

In quiet moments, whispers flow,
Softly guiding where we go.
In tender love, the spirit speaks,
Through gentle sighs, our hearts it seeks.

With every breeze, a hint of grace,
In nature's arms, we find our place.
The still small voice, our doubts assuage,
Encouraging us to turn the page.

Through trials faced and choices made,
In gentle whispers, we're not afraid.
Connected souls, a bond so pure,
In faith we find the holy cure.

When darkness looms, and hope feels lost,
These whispers remind us of the cost.
Through loss and pain, His love remains,
In every heart, the truth sustains.

So listen close, let silence speak,
In gentle whispers, strength we seek.
For in those moments, love prevails,
Embracing us through life's travails.

Building Bridges with the Divine

In silence deep, our spirits rise,
We reach for grace across the skies.
With open hearts, we seek to find,
The sacred bond that ties our kind.

With gentle hands, we build the way,
Toward light that breaks the dawn of day.
Through faith and love, our paths align,
In trust, we walk, the world divine.

Each step a prayer, each breath a song,
Together, where we all belong.
In grace, we find our truest face,
And work to heal this wounded place.

Embrace the hands that join with ours,
In unity, we seek the powers.
With every bridge that we create,
We join in love, we celebrate.

Oh wondrous light, our guiding star,
Through trials faced, we've come this far.
With open arms, we welcome in,
The peace that blooms where love begins.

The Quiet Revolution of the Soul

In the stillness, whispers grow,
A revolution, soft and slow.
Where hearts awaken, shadows flee,
An inner light sets spirit free.

Through humble paths, the truth will shine,
Each step a chance to redefine.
In quiet spaces, courage found,
A sacred song, a holy sound.

With every breath, the world transforms,
In gentleness, the spirit warms.
Unfolding like a blossomed rose,
The power of our love bestows.

In unity, we stand as one,
The quiet vow of hearts begun.
With every tear, a seed is sown,
In softness, deeper roots are grown.

As walls fall down, and hearts unite,
The dawn of hope, a blessed light.
In humbleness, we find our whole,
A quiet revolution of the soul.

An Offering of Restoration

In brokenness, we find the grace,
A gentle hand to heal the place.
Through every wound, a chance to mend,
An offering of love we send.

In whispered prayers, our hopes reside,
With faith, we turn our hearts to guide.
In sacred stillness, peace will bloom,
Restoration blooms where love's in tune.

With every breath, we breathe anew,
An offering for me and you.
In gratitude, we lift our voice,
In unity, we make the choice.

To let go pain, embrace the light,
In brokenness, we find our sight.
Through trials faced, our strength revealed,
Together, hearts and souls are healed.

With open hearts, we share the load,
An offering as we walk this road.
Each moment cherished, love's affection,
In every step, the sweet connection.

The Softening of the Soul

In gentle light, our hearts unfold,
A tender touch, a story told.
The softening of edges worn,
In love's embrace, we are reborn.

Through hurts and trials, wisdom grows,
In quiet moments, spirit flows.
With every breath, a chance to heal,
The softness blooms, our truth revealed.

In sacred stillness, joy will rise,
A melody within the skies.
With open arms, we greet the dawn,
In softening grace, we carry on.

Through every tear, a chance to learn,
With hearts aflame, our spirits burn.
The gentle call of peace will guide,
The softening of the soul inside.

Together, hand in hand we roam,
In every heart, we find our home.
In soft whispers, love's refrain,
The softening of soul remains.

The Sacred Path of Renewal

In the stillness of dawn's light,
Whispers of grace take flight.
Footsteps on the sacred ground,
Where peace and love abound.

Each breath a gift from above,
Wrapping the heart in holy love.
The spirit blooms, fresh and free,
In the hands of divinity.

Through trials we learn to believe,
In each lesson, we receive.
Cleansed by fire, we rise anew,
With faith, our colors shine true.

Kindness flows like a gentle stream,
United by a common dream.
With humble hearts, we seek to share,
The sacred path of earnest prayer.

In twilight's glow, shadows will fade,
As we walk, our fears invade.
Yet through the night, stars will guide,
On this journey, we abide.

When Tears Become a Prayer

In the silence, sorrow spills,
Washing over life's vast hills.
Each tear a message sent above,
A testament of hope and love.

When burdens seem too hard to bear,
We find solace in whispered prayer.
Each droplet, a sacred cry,
Reaches the heavens, soaring high.

The heartache melts like morning frost,
In every loss, not all is lost.
For from the depths, new strength will flow,
From grief, the sweetest blossoms grow.

With faith, we learn to rise again,
To dance in storms, to embrace the rain.
Through shattered dreams, we find our way,
When tears become a prayer each day.

In the tapestry of life's plight,
Love stitches shadows into light.
For every tear that falls in pain,
Is a seed of joy that can remain.

The Soul's Resilient Journey

Through valleys low and mountains high,
The soul's resolve will never die.
Each step unfolds a sacred tale,
Guided by faith, we shall prevail.

In the mirror of time's embrace,
We search for strength, we seek his grace.
With every hardship that we face,
The spirit grows in boundless space.

As rivers flow to the mighty sea,
So too does love set our hearts free.
Through storms and trials, spirits dance,
In every moment, we take a chance.

The wanderer's heart knows no end,
In shadows deep, we find a friend.
With lessons learned, we rise once more,
The soul's resilient journey, we explore.

In the tapestry of night and day,
Hope shines brighter, come what may.
For every journey leads us home,
In the heart, we are never alone.

In the Embrace of Hope

When darkness looms, and fear takes hold,
In hope's embrace, we become bold.
Every heartbeat, a song of light,
Guiding us through the endless night.

In whispers soft, the spirit speaks,
With every sigh, our essence seeks.
The dawn will break, the shadows flee,
In the embrace of hope, we see.

The path ahead may twist and turn,
Yet with each step, our spirits learn.
Every moment, a chance to rise,
In the heart's depths, love never dies.

Through trials faced, we find our strength,
In kindness shared, we go great lengths.
With open hearts, we choose to trust,
In the embrace of hope, we must.

For life's a journey, vast and wide,
In every heart, a spark to guide.
Together, we weave a world anew,
In the embrace of hope, we pursue.

A Sacred Return to Joy

In the garden of grace, we find our way,
Where laughter and love are here to stay.
Hearts intertwined in the sunlight's glow,
A sacred return, let our spirits grow.

With whispers of mercy guiding us near,
We dance through the shadows, casting off fear.
The rhythm of faith beats strong in our chest,
In the arms of the Father, we find our rest.

Rejoice in the moments, both humble and grand,
Each heartbeat a blessing, each touch a hand.
Together we rise, let our joy be unfurled,
In this sacred return, we embrace the world.

The heavens are cheering, the angels align,
With every new dawn, His love we define.
In this holy place, we forge our own way,
A sacred return to joy, come what may.

Echoes of Faith in the Night

In the silence of night, God's whispers arise,
Stars like His promises fill up the skies.
The shadows may whisper, but faith is the light,
In echoes of truth, darkness takes flight.

With courage we walk through the valleys of doubt,
His love is a beacon; it helps us stand stout.
In every heartache, His grace is our guide,
In echoes of faith, we boldly abide.

Though storms may rattle, we anchor in prayer,
In moments of stillness, His presence is there.
The night may be long, yet joy will ignite,
Through echoes of faith, we awaken our sight.

Together we stand in this sacred embrace,
Finding hope in the trials, our fears we replace.
With each gentle dawn, a new day takes flight,
In echoes of faith, we banish the night.

Wings of Forgiveness

In the garden of healing, we learn to forgive,
With each gentle breath, a new way to live.
Let go of the burdens that weigh on our soul,
On wings of forgiveness, we find ourselves whole.

The past may linger, its shadows may call,
Yet love is the answer, it conquers all.
In the light of His mercy, our hearts find peace,
With wings of forgiveness, our pain will cease.

Embrace one another, let kindness prevail,
In the warmth of compassion, no heart shall fail.
We rise above trials, together in flight,
With wings of forgiveness, we shine ever bright.

In the tapestry woven with threads of our grace,
Each act of love, a sacred embrace.
So spread forth your wings and let your heart soar,
On the wings of forgiveness, we heal and restore.

The Altar of Resilience

At the altar of resilience, we gather in strength,
With stories of struggle stretching our length.
Through fires that forge us and storms that refine,
In the heart of our faith, together we shine.

With each hurdle faced, our spirits adorn,
The battles we fought, in the light they are born.
We rise from the ashes, renewed in our fight,
At the altar of resilience, we find our light.

Together in prayer, we nurture our dreams,
With hands held in hope, we flow like the streams.
Every scar tells a story, each wound made us wise,
At the altar of resilience, our hearts learn to rise.

In unity strong, we gather and share,
The power of granting, the courage to care.
As one, we remember the love that ignites,
At the altar of resilience, we soar to new heights.

The Fortress of Forgiveness

In shadows deep, love's light shall shine,
A refuge found where hearts align.
In whispers soft, grace does abide,
Forgiveness blooms, the soul's true guide.

When burdens weigh, and spirits fall,
In mercy's arms, we answer the call.
With every tear, a lesson learned,
In the fortress built, our hearts returned.

Embrace the pain, let go the strife,
In the sacred space, we find new life.
The past released, like autumn leaves,
In forgiveness' light, our spirit believes.

Through trials faced and battles fought,
In the depths of soul, compassion is sought.
With open hands, we mend the seams,
In the fortress of love, we weave our dreams.

Here in the silence, the soul takes flight,
Forging a bond that feels so right.
We walk the path where kindness leads,
In the warmth of grace, our spirit feeds.

Divine Alchemy of the Soul

In sacred fire, the spirit brews,
Transforming pain, a vibrant muse.
With whispered prayers, and hearts ablaze,
We find the gold in shifting ways.

Each trial faced, a lesson's birth,
In the cosmic dance, we find our worth.
Through shadows dark, illumination grows,
In transformation's grace, our essence glows.

The elixir flows, pure and bright,
In the alchemy of love's pure light.
A vessel true, our souls entwined,
In divine union, pure hearts aligned.

In sacred stillness, we resonate,
With every beat, we elevate.
The burdens shed, clarity brings,
In the sacred dance, the soul finds wings.

Through trials we rise, and faith ignites,
In the heart's embrace, we soar to heights.
With love's embrace, we are made whole,
In divine alchemy, we've found our role.

The Uplifted Heart

In gentle grace, the heart takes flight,
With hope renewed, through darkest night.
Each beat a prayer, a song of peace,
In love's embrace, our fears release.

The mountain high, the valley low,
In every storm, the spirit grows.
With every step, we find our way,
In the uplifted heart, we choose to stay.

In moments still, the truth revealed,
From brokenness, our wounds are healed.
With open arms, we gather near,
In unity's strength, we have no fear.

Through laughter shared and tears we shed,
In fellowship, our souls are fed.
With kindness shown, and love imparted,
The uplifted heart remains unguarded.

In every breath, we rise anew,
With hearts aflame, and spirits true.
Together bound by love's sweet grace,
In the uplifted heart, we find our place.

Sanctity in Suffering

In shadows cast, the spirit yearns,
Through trials faced, the heart still burns.
In every tear, a sacred sigh,
Amidst the pain, our spirits fly.

Each struggle holds a deeper truth,
A pathway forged, returning youth.
In suffering's grip, we find our might,
A holy fire ignites the night.

The sacred scars, they tell our tale,
In brokenness, our spirits sail.
With every wound, a lesson learned,
In suffering's depth, our souls are turned.

Through valleys low and mountains high,
In trials faced, we reach for the sky.
With faith as guide, we choose to stand,
In sanctity found, we understand.

In whispered prayers, the heart abides,
In suffering's embrace, love never hides.
With open hearts, we walk this road,
In the sanctity of pain, our strength bestowed.

The Promise of Dawn's Embrace

In the silence of night, hope takes flight,
A whispering breeze, guiding the light.
The stars gently fade, love's soft embrace,
Promising joy in the dawn's warm face.

With every new day, grace fills the sky,
Washing away tears, as time drifts by.
Faith blossoms bright, as shadows recede,
In the heart's garden, where souls are freed.

Each sunrise a canvas, splashed with gold,
Stories of courage and love retold.
Awakened spirits, rising from slumber,
Finding their strength in hope's sweet number.

A journey begins at the break of morn,
With promises kept, and new life reborn.
In unity bound, we dance and we sing,
As dawn's gentle embrace, our spirits bring.

Together we stand, under heavens wide,
Embracing the light, with faith as our guide.
Hand in hand we walk, through valleys and streams,
In the promise of dawn, we find our dreams.

From Ashes, We Ascend

When shadows fall deep, and night seems long,
The heart finds its voice, in an ancient song.
From embers we rise, with courage anew,
Touched by the grace of the morning dew.

With faith as our armor, we face the blaze,
Transforming our trials into praises raised.
What once had been broken shall come to be,
A tapestry woven in unity.

In the depth of despair, a seed is sown,
Through struggle and pain, our spirits have grown.
From ashes we build, a temple of light,
Guided by love, through the dark of night.

Hope flickers and shines, like stars in the void,
Each challenge embraced, every fear destroyed.
With wings of the spirit, we learn to ascend,
In the arms of compassion, our wounds shall mend.

Together we rise, as one we will soar,
From ashes to heights, where we all can explore.
In the beauty of pain, we find our release,
For from ashes we rise, and in love, we find peace.

The Dawn of Healing Light

In the hush of the morn, a promise unfolds,
With whispers of hope, as the new day molds.
The dawn casts a glow on wounds that we bear,
Healing each heart in its tender care.

With each gentle ray that breaks through the dark,
A symphony starts, a resonant spark.
The light soars within, transforming our pain,
Renewing the spirit, like soft, falling rain.

Through valleys of sorrow, the light will lead,
A compass of love, where our souls are freed.
Through trials we journey, hand in hand we strive,
In the dawn of our healing, we come alive.

As shadows retreat and the truth is revealed,
A tapestry woven, our scars are healed.
In unity strong, we gather as one,
Embracing the warmth of a new rising sun.

With faith as our anchor, we rise, we ignite,
In the strength of our love, we find our true light.
Together we stand at the break of today,
In the dawn of our healing, we pave our own way.

A Graceful Rebirth

In the stillness of time, we breathe anew,
A graceful rebirth, in the morning dew.
Each moment is sacred, a chance to grow,
From ashes we rise, to the light we sow.

With hearts open wide, we welcome the change,
In the garden of life, where all feels strange.
The winds of the spirit carry us high,
In the dance of rebirth, we dare to fly.

Through trials we wander, our fears laid bare,
In the arms of the Divine, we find our care.
Letting go of the past, we embrace the now,
With gratitude deep, we humbly bow.

Each sunbeam a promise, each shadow a guide,
In the circle of life, where love will abide.
We find our true selves, in the rhythm of grace,
In the tapestry woven, every thread has its place.

Together we flourish, in harmony's song,
Embracing the journey, where we all belong.
With hope as our beacon, we rise from the dark,
In the light of rebirth, we find our true spark.

Songs of Hope in the Wilderness

In the heart of despair, a whisper grows,
From the depths of the earth, a sweet song flows.
Beneath the shadows, a light appears,
Guiding the lost through their darkest fears.

Mountains high, valleys low, a journey we take,
With faith as our compass, and love, the path we make.
Each step we tread, in grace we find,
A hymn of the spirit, in unity entwined.

The weary traveler sings a tune,
In the glow of dawn, beneath the silver moon.
Voices unite, echoing the call,
In the wilderness, we rise, we shall not fall.

Every tear shed waters the ground,
In trials of life, strength is found.
Hope is the anchor, steadfast and true,
In the wilderness, He leads us through.

Lift your eyes, for the dawn is near,
In the songs of hope, dispel every fear.
Together we soar, on wings of grace,
In the wilderness, we find our place.

Threads of Faith and Healing

In the fabric of life, threads intertwine,
Each stitch a prayer, each knot divine.
Woven with love, through trials and tears,
A tapestry brightens with hopes and fears.

With every heartbeat, a promise is made,
In the silence of night, our doubts will fade.
Gentle hands mend the wounds we bear,
In the warmth of compassion, we find hope there.

Through shadows we wander, yet not alone,
For in every struggle, His light has shone.
Bridges of faith, strong and tall,
Guide us together, answering the call.

Time is a healer, though slow it may be,
In faith's soft embrace, we learn to see.
Each moment a gift, a chance to behold,
The beauty in trials, a story retold.

So let us gather, in circles of grace,
Sharing our stories, finding our place.
In the threads of healing, we weave and mend,
Together in spirit, on love we depend.

The Radiance Beyond Sorrow

In the depths of sorrow, a glimmer shines,
Hope flickers gently, like sacred signs.
Through the trials faced, pain can reshape,
Our hearts into vessels of faith and escape.

When shadows linger and darkness encroaches,
The soul finds solace in love that approaches.
Count every blessing, in laughter and strife,
For beauty emerges, rebirthing life.

The stars above guide us through night's embrace,
With each twinkling light, feel the warm grace.
Step forward in trust, let your heart soar,
The radiance beckons, forevermore.

And when sorrow speaks with its heavy hand,
Listen closely, for there's wisdom at hand.
Every tear shed holds a story profound,
In the depths of loss, new purpose is found.

Awake to the morning, breathe deeply the air,
In every heartbeat, know love is there.
The radiance beyond sorrow ignites the flame,
Bringing us closer, reminding us of His name.

Finding Peace in the Chaos

In the whirlwind of life, where stillness feels rare,
Seek the quiet moments, the balm of prayer.
When storms rise fierce, and troubles invade,
In faith, we discover the peace, unafraid.

Beneath the chaos, a river flows calm,
A sanctuary found, in love's gentle balm.
Hold onto hope when the world feels vast,
For peace isn't fleeting; it's meant to last.

In the frenzy of day, carve moments to rest,
Cling to the truths that nurture the blessed.
Every breath taken becomes a new chance,
To dance in the chaos, in life's wild dance.

Let not the noise drown the whispers within,
For in stillness of heart, true harmony begins.
Each trial faced becomes the song of our soul,
In finding our peace, we become whole.

So gather your thoughts, embrace the unknown,
In the chaos of life, we're never alone.
Let grace be the anchor, the light, and the guide,
Finding peace in the chaos, with faith as our pride.

Wings of Resurgence

High above the sorrowed earth,
Angels stir with love rebirth.
Soaring on the winds of grace,
Hope embraces every space.

In the dawn, a promise shines,
In each heart, the spirit binds.
Lift us up, O gentle light,
Guide our souls to radiant height.

From despair, a path unfolds,
Through the trials, truth consoles.
Wings of faith shall carry wide,
In our hearts, love shall reside.

With every tear, a seed we sow,
In the garden, faith shall grow.
Together, we shall rise anew,
In the light, our spirits true.

Awakened by the dawn's embrace,
United in our sacred space.
Wings of resurgence, lift us high,
To the realms where angels fly.

Cradling the Fragments

In the quiet night we find,
Pieces of our hearts entwined.
Cradled softly by His hand,
Hearts transformed, anew we stand.

Scattered dreams like stars above,
Gathered in the arms of love.
Mending wounds with tender grace,
We are held in His embrace.

Shadows whisper, hope appears,
Cleansing all our hidden fears.
Each fragment tells a sacred tale,
Through His mercy, we prevail.

Time shall weave a sacred song,
Binding us, forever strong.
With every breath, the light we seek,
In our bones, His love we speak.

Together in this holy dance,
Cradling hope, we find our chance.
From brokenness, a vessel pure,
In His grace, we shall endure.

Sacred Reawakening

In the hush of morning light,
Souls arise from endless night.
Awakened by a soft refrain,
Life renewed, released from pain.

Voices echo through the trees,
Whispers riding on the breeze.
Nature sings a hymn of peace,
In the stillness, doubts release.

Hearts aligned, a sacred call,
In His love, we find our all.
Every breath a gift divine,
In this moment, we align.

From the ashes, hope shall soar,
Boundless joy forevermore.
Every shadow, every tear,
Fades away as love draws near.

In the depths of silence found,
Holy echoes all around.
Sacred reawakening,
In each heart, new life will spring.

From Grief, a Hymn

In the depths where shadows dwell,
From the heart, a silent well.
Grief weaves through the sacred song,
In the sorrow, we belong.

Each tear falls like sacred rain,
Nurturing the soul's deep pain.
In our mourning, strength we find,
A hymn of heart, forever kind.

Brokenness can lead us home,
Through the night, no need to roam.
Voices rise, a chorus clear,
Each heartbeat, drawing near.

The chords of loss are bittersweet,
In our hearts, His love repeats.
From the ashes of despair,
A melody, beyond compare.

In remembrance, we shall sing,
Life transformed, we take to wing.
From grief, a hymn shall rise,
Carried forth to endless skies.

The Garden of Second Chances

Amidst the blooms of hope, we stand,
Seeking refuge from the land.
In every petal, mercy's spark,
Nature whispers through the dark.

In our hearts, the seeds are sown,
Nurtured grace, we've always known.
With every breath, we find our way,
In the light of a brand new day.

The past may haunt, but here we grow,
Forgiving shadows, letting go.
In this garden, life begins anew,
On paths of faith, we wander through.

Lifting burdens, casting fears,
Every tear becomes a sphere.
Through the soil of love, we thrive,
In the warmth of grace, we are alive.

With every sunrise, hope appears,
A chorus sung throughout the years.
In the garden of our souls,
Divine mercy makes us whole.

Divine Mercy Unfolding

In the stillness of the night,
Whispers of grace take their flight.
Upon the heart, a gentle touch,
Love that heals, love that's such.

From the heavens comes a call,
In our weakness, we stand tall.
With each step upon this earth,
We find in pain, a holy birth.

Let the light within us shine,
Every soul, a thread divine.
In the tapestry of fate,
We discover love's true weight.

Through the trials and the strife,
Behold, the mercy of true life.
With open hands, we receive grace,
In the warmth of love's embrace.

Together we walk, heart to heart,
In the dance of love, we part.
With every blessing, joy will swell,
In divine mercy, all is well.

Rise Like the Morning Star

Awake, O heart, the dawn is near,
With shining hope, let go of fear.
As morning breaks with golden rays,
We rise anew, we sing His praise.

Upon the horizon, grace unfolds,
In whispers soft, the truth beholds.
Through shadows cast, we learn to soar,
With every trial, we seek for more.

Lift your eyes to skies so wide,
In faith's embrace, we will abide.
As dawn renews the weary soul,
In the light, we become whole.

With every heartbeat, joy ignites,
The promise shines through starry nights.
From ashes, beauty is restored,
In love's embrace, we are adored.

So rise, dear spirit, and take your flight,
Transforming darkness into light.
With each step on this sacred road,
We walk with Him, our heavy load.

Through Darkness into Grace

In shadows deep, we search for peace,
Yearning hearts find sweet release.
Through trials faced, we come to know,
In every tear, His love will flow.

When burdens weigh upon our souls,
In silent whispers, love consoles.
Through valleys low, we tread with care,
Faith guides us onward, everywhere.

We lift our gaze to skies above,
In every breath, we find His love.
Through darkness deep, we shed our fears,
In grace, we find our way through tears.

For every step, a promise made,
In every heart, His light displayed.
Through trials faced, we learn to rise,
With faithful hearts, we touch the skies.

So walk with courage, take the chance,
In the rhythm of divine dance.
Through darkness into grace, we stride,
In love's embrace, we shall abide.

The Prayer of the Suffering

In shadows deep, we plead for grace,
A whisper soft, in this dark place.
Oh Lord, hear our weary sighs,
Lift us up to brighter skies.

With every ache, our spirits yearn,
In faith we trust, for love's return.
Your mercy flows like healing rain,
Restore our hearts, erase the pain.

Through trials faced, we seek the light,
In the depths, You are our sight.
Guide our steps on paths unknown,
In Your embrace, we are not alone.

Grant us peace, a gentle balm,
In restless nights, bring us calm.
Let our burdens, together, share,
As we rise up in fervent prayer.

In suffering's trial, we shall find,
The strength of heart, the peace of mind.
Through every tear, our souls will grow,
In Your love, we are made whole.

Sunrise in the Valley of Tears

In valleys low, where sorrows dwell,
The dawn breaks softly, a sacred spell.
Light spills over the hills so near,
A promise whispered, do not fear.

Each tear spilled is a seed of grace,
In the rich soil, life finds its place.
God's tender hand wipes every face,
For from sorrow, joy will embrace.

The sun ascends with gentle might,
Casting warmth on the weary night.
In the silence, hope takes flight,
The heart awakens, bathed in light.

Nature sings in vibrant hues,
As faith ignites in morning's muse.
In every shadow, the light breaks through,
Reviving dreams, making all things new.

Let not the past define the day,
For each sunrise paves a new way.
Embrace the dawn, let your heart steer,
In the valley of tears, love draws near.

Testament of the Forgiven

With heavy hearts, we bear our shame,
But in Your love, we find our name.
You cleanse our souls, a pure embrace,
Forgiveness blooms, a sacred space.

Let go of chains that held us tight,
In mercy's glow, we claim the light.
Each wound healed by grace divine,
In open arms, our spirits shine.

Forgiveness flows like rivers strong,
In unity, we all belong.
Together we rise, from sin released,
In humble hearts, we find our peace.

Remember not our wrongs, we plead,
For in Your love, we are freed.
Let compassion guide our hands,
As we fulfill Your holy plans.

In every heart, a story told,
Of grace received and love extolled.
We stand as one, our vow confirmed,
The testament of hearts now warmed.

The Sacred Art of Letting Go

In quiet moments, we release,
The burdens held, embracing peace.
With gentle hands, we open wide,
The cage of fear, in truth, we bide.

Let go of dreams that serve no end,
For in surrender, we transcend.
The past can't guide, nor shape the now,
In faith we trust, as we avow.

The heart in stillness finds its song,
In every breath, where we belong.
Letting go brings a sacred gift,
A liberating, soulful lift.

With every tear, a lesson learned,
In letting go, our hearts have turned.
To love anew, to trust the flow,
In this sacred art of letting go.

In open hands, the world unfolds,
In whispered prayers, the heart beholds.
Freedom awaits, just take the leap,
In letting go, our souls will keep.

Covenant of Healing

In faith we gather, hearts entwined,
The promise of peace, divinely signed.
With hands extended, grace pours forth,
A healing touch, a holy birth.

Sickness fades in whispered prayer,
In unity, we lay our care.
The spirit mends what once was broken,
In this sacred bond, hope is spoken.

Through trials faced, we find our way,
The light of love will guide our stay.
In every tear, a seed is sown,
A covenant made, we're not alone.

So let us walk, hand in hand,
In life's embrace, we take our stand.
The promise of healing flows like a stream,
In the arms of faith, we dare to dream.

With grateful hearts, we raise our song,
In the name of love, we all belong.
The covenant stands, ever so true,
In this sacred space, we're made anew.

The Pilgrim's Return

A journey long, through storm and night,
Hope guides the steps toward the light.
With weary hearts, to home we go,
In faith's embrace, our spirits grow.

The path was rough, the road was long,
Yet in our hearts, we sing a song.
For every trial, a lesson learned,
In every shadow, the soul returned.

The shelter found in sacred ground,
In every prayer, love's echo found.
With arms outstretched, we greet the morn,
A fellowship of hearts reborn.

With grateful steps, we walk in peace,
In faith's embrace, our fears release.
The homecoming, a sacred rite,
In love's embrace, we find our light.

So let us gather, lift our praise,
In joyous hearts, our spirits raise.
The pilgrimage leads us back to grace,
In every moment, we find our place.

Light Breaks Through

When darkest hour seems to reign,
A flicker of hope breaks the chain.
In silent whispers, angels sing,
The dawn of peace, a sacred thing.

Beneath the veil of tears and strife,
There flows a stream, the gift of life.
Through every heart, a light will shine,
In brokenness, the love divine.

The shadows dance, but cannot stay,
For light ignites the path to sway.
In every soul, a fire glows,
A beacon bright, where mercy flows.

Through trials faced, we rise anew,
In unity, the heart breaks through.
With arms uplifted, we stand tall,
In hope's embrace, we heed the call.

So let the light within us beam,
In darkest nights, we dare to dream.
Together bound, we stride in love,
In light's embrace, we rise above.

A New Song of the Spirit

In every heartbeat lies a song,
A melody where we belong.
The spirit sings, a joyous tune,
In hearts awakened, night turns to noon.

With every breath, the chorus swells,
In harmony, the spirit dwells.
So lift your voice, let praises soar,
In love's embrace, forevermore.

In trials faced, we find our strength,
In unity, we go the length.
Each story woven, thread divine,
A tapestry of love, we find.

The spirit guides, through darkest times,
In whispered prayers, our hope climbs.
Through every challenge, we hold fast,
With faith's assurance, fears are cast.

With grateful hearts, let songs arise,
In every note, our spirits fly.
In this new dawn, together sing,
A love eternal, the spirit brings.

Milton Keynes UK
Ingram Content Group UK Ltd.
UKHW031321271124
451618UK00007B/145